Bean has an empty tin.
He puts it in a bin.

Bean cuts his chin on the rim.
Jelly comes to look at him.

But Jelly stands on a pin.
Oh no! The pin is in her skin.

She jumps up in a spin ... and she lands on her chin.

A lump comes up on Jelly's chin.
Bean helps her with the pin.

'You look silly with that chin,'
said Bean to Jelly, with a grin.

Jelly and Bean go to the bin.
They have a look for the tin.

The tin is not in the bin.
But Jelly can see a big pin!